THE
NATIONAL PARKS
OF THE ROCKIES

The publishers would like to express their thanks to all the officials of the National Park Service who so kindly assisted them in the production of this book. In particular, they acknowledge with gratitude the permission of E. Patrick Smith, Chief Ranger Naturalist of Grand Teton National Park, to use his text in the section on Grand Teton National Park.

THE NATIONAL PARKS OF THE ROCKIES

Text by
James V. Murfin

Introduction by
Bill Harris

CRESCENT BOOKS
NEW YORK

Introduction

Back in 1920, long after Yellowstone, Glacier, the Grand Canyon and a dozen more National Parks had been established in the West, the Camp Fire Club of America decided it was time to declare what a National Park actually was. They are "spacious land and water areas of nationwide interest established as inviolable sanctuaries for the permanent preservation of scenery, wilderness and native flora and fauna in their natural condition." It's a definition that still applies after all those years. But even by 1920 the scenery, wilderness and life within the boundaries of the Parks that had already been established was varied enough to prompt the Club to add to its list that a National Park was a place of "unique inspirational beauty."

How else could a place with the rugged, Alpine majesty of Glacier National Park be put into the same category as the Indian cliff dwellings at Mesa Verde, or the fossilized barrier reef that is preserved at Guadalupe Mountains Park in West Texas?

The same reef that surrounded an inland sea some 250 million years ago is also responsible for Carlsbad Caverns in New Mexico, but all they have in common today is that they're both National Parks. The broad valley that stretches out eastward from the Grand Tetons allows visitors to that National Park to stand back in awe of them, but most don't climb to the top of any of the peaks. On the other hand, the experience of Rocky Mountain National Park is lost on anyone who doesn't go to the top of the Continental Divide to look down instead of up.

The deserts and canyons of Big Bend National Park, straddling the border between Texas and Mexico, are nothing at all like the mesas and canyons at Canyonlands Park in Utah, or the rock formations a few miles away at Arches National Park. And Utah's Bryce Canyon more nearly resembles the great Grand Canyon in Arizona, though nothing on earth is quite like the magnificent, mile-deep cut that has become one of the most easily recognized symbols of America.

People who have never had the pleasure of sitting on a wooden bench waiting for the plume of steam and hot water that is Old Faithful geyser in Yellowstone Park know exactly what it looks like. It has been a symbol of America since before Yellowstone became America's first National Park back in 1872. Yet, like the Grand Canyon, there is nothing else anywhere in America quite like it.

The layer of limestone that forms the upper walls of the Grand Canyon extends northward into Utah and Zion National Park, which became part of the park system in 1919, the same year as the Grand Canyon. But the bright colored rocks of Zion seem more rugged, the countryside wilder. And neither would ever be confused with the desert rocks of Capitol Reef, named for the dome-like formations that resemble the architecture of capitol buildings.

And different from all of them is Arizona's Petrified Forest, the largest deposit of wood turned to stone in the world. Together with the Painted Desert, it is one of the most colorful of the National Parks. But it has very little in common with any of the others.

And that is what makes America's National Park system such a wonderful thing. Though several are within a few miles of one another, each and every one of them has its own distinct personality. Almost no one ever drives through Yellowstone without spending at least a day admiring the Grand Tetons. And if the same visitors miss Glacier Park to the north or Rocky Mountain Park to the south, they have good reasons to go back.

When the Camp Fire Club set about defining National Parks more than a half century ago, they pointed out that the essence of the system should be areas "without interference from man-made distractions." Back in those days the automobile was a simple affair, motels hadn't been thought of and billboards were a long way in the future. The pace was slower and fast food outlets unthinkable. But in spite of the possible encroachment of such things in the years since, the National Parks have managed to stay what they were intended to be. Among the things they were intended to be is a legacy for our children. We are the children of the men who established the legacy, holding these fragile landscapes in trust for the future.

They are more than living museums, more than glimpses of a world that civilization seems rushing headlong to destroy. Their diversity needs to be saved. In much of the United States, vacationers cruising down the Interstates can't find any difference from one town to another, or from one Interstate to another for that matter. The strings of motels, self-service filling stations, convenience stores and fast food outlets are the same at every exit. But no one could ever mistake one National Park for another. It's what makes them such a wonderful resource for every American, and nowhere in America is the resource as abundant as west and south of the Continental Divide.

Grand Teton National Park

Les Trois Tetons!

Towering more than a mile above the valley known as Jackson Hole, the Grand Teton reaches an elevation of 13,770 feet above sea level. Surrounding the Grand Teton are six additional peaks that rise above 12,000 feet. Collectively, these peaks and others close by form the Teton Range, one of the most spectacular mountain ranges in North America. The creation of this impressive landscape is a classic example of a fairly common mountain building process: block faulting.

Beginning approximately ten million years ago, considerably later than the formation of much of the Rocky Mountain chain some 40-50 million years previously, two blocks of earth began to separate along a 40 mile fracture in the earth's crust. Described in terms that are easy to visualize, these two rectangular blocks moved like giant trap doors. One gigantic block was pushed skyward to form the mountains; the other hinged downward to form the valley floor. This separation process occurred in many different stages, with the blocks being uplifted or depressed from a few inches to a few feet each time they slid by one another.

The geological process that formed the Teton Range is far from over: the scene is not finished. Current scientific evidence indicates that the mountains are being uplifted, the valley floor depressed, and the glaciers are still eroding canyons. No one can say what the future vista of Grand Teton will be; only that in upcoming geological time it will be different.

The arrival of humans on the scene has been only in recent geological time. Sometime between nine and ten thousand years ago, shortly after the retreat of the last valley glaciers, native Americans migrated into the valley. They were following the large herds of wandering mammals – elk, bison and bighorn sheep – as they summered on the valley floor and in mountain canyons. Due to the harsh environment, the bitterly cold temperatures, deep snow and lack of food, it is doubtful that the early people wintered in the valley, and their possible descendents, the Shoshoni, Crow, Bannock, Nez Perce and Gros Ventre tribes, continued this migratory hunting-gathering tradition until the arrival of the fur trade era.

The beaver was responsible for the first surge of exploration in the western wilderness, for it was the highly-prized fur of this animal, used in the east and in Europe to make men's hats, that lured trappers into the west in search of fortune. One of the early trappers, David E. Jackson, became fond of the valley beneath the Tetons and so, in the tradition of the trappers, this high mountain valley, or "hole," became Jackson's Hole. It was some time later that the possessive was dropped and it became Jackson Hole.

Jackson Hole developed into a crossroads for the fur trade, but its heyday was short-lived. Fashion in Europe changed, silk hats became the vogue, and the beaver, close to being wiped out in the west, was given a reprieve. Loss of habitat, however, meant that the animal would never return to its former numbers.

After the fur trappers departed, Jackson Hole was seldom visited until the 1870s, when the U.S. Geological Survey began to map the West. Their reports of the spectacular thermal features to the north of Grand Teton led to the establishment of the nation's first national park, Yellowstone, in 1872. But the impressive mountain range, the massive granite peaks, were not included in this park.

In 1929 Congress voted to establish Grant Teton National Park. The newly-created park contained only the peaks and piedmont lakes, and not the valley floor. In 1927 John D. Rockefeller, Jr. formed the Snake River Land Company, which purchased over 30,000 acres in the valley during the next 20 years. President Franklin D. Roosevelt created the Jackson Hole Monument which consisted of most federal land in Jackson Hole in 1943. The government accepted Rockefeller's donation in 1949, and in 1950 the Monument and original Park were combined to form the present boundaries of Grand Teton National Park.

The great peaks of the Teton Range and the valley floor of Jackson Hole provide outstanding habitat for many species of wildlife. One of the world's largest elk herds resides in Jackson Hole. Moose, mule deer, black bear, beaver, and coyote are among the species that can be found in the park.

The wonders of this National Park are many. Mountains, wildlife, rivers, canyons and valley all contribute to make this one of the nation's most spectacular parks.

Arches National Park and Canyonlands National Park

It is a lovely and terrible wilderness ...harshly and beautifully colored, broken and worn until its bones are exposed, its great sky without a smudge or taint from Technocracy, and in hidden corners and pockets under its cliffs the sudden poetry of springs.
Wallace Stegner, *The Sound of Mountain Water*

Utah, Arizona, New Mexico, Colorado. Four Corners. The Colorado Plateau. The land of canyons.

The Colorado Plateau is an island of flat-lying rock between the Rocky Mountains and the deserts of the West: a high, flat table, dotted here and there with isolated, snow-capped peaks and laced with an interconnecting, rugged and dramatic scenery that sweeps the mind with shapes and colors. This is nature's hideaway, seemingly forbidden to man and beast alike. Water created this plateau, and it is water that has eaten into its heart and slowly, inexorably taken it away. Nowhere is this erosion more dramatically demonstrated than in the southeast corner of Utah at Arches and Canyonlands National Parks.

The mighty Colorado River, flowing from the east, meets its tributary, the Green River, flowing from the north, in the heart of Canyonlands National Park. Together they shape, as they have done longer than man knows, the most incredible examples of water erosion on the earth: there's nothing else like it anywhere. And it is a monstrous task to describe. "I would describe Canyonlands as the place where the adjective died from exhaustion," wrote Freeman Tilden. He was right. Even those who attempted to name the formations relied on the noun: Bagpipe Butte, Elephant Canyon, Devil's Lane, The Sewing Machine, The Doll House. There are arches, pillars, needles, spires, pinnacles, domes, steeples, and hundreds of others that need only the eye and a vivid imagination. Massive sandstone columns stand like skyscrapers. Angel Arch has an opening 190 feet high under which could sit the Arc de Triomphe, with some 16 feet to spare. And some of this is still unexplored. What great sights await those hardy souls who will venture beyond the trails!

The scenery in Arches National Park, just to the north of Moab and only a short distance from Canyonlands, is every bit as spectacular. This small park – small in comparison to Canyonlands, but huge in its array of geological formations - lies on the north bank of the Colorado River as it passes into Utah. Here is a phenomenal collection of natural arches, windows, spires, rocks balanced precariously on rocks - the most concentrated assemblage in the country.

This park takes its name from the dominant feature, natural stone arches so delicately formed that one marvels at their stability, fearing to walk beneath lest they crack and crumble. Landscape Arch is considered the longest in the world; it spans 291 feet and at one point is only six feet thick. No engineer could successfully duplicate it, yet nature in its infinite wisdom has been master architect.

Over 400 arches have been found in this red-rock country and, no doubt, others have escaped the eye. This is sandstone - sand deposited 150 million years ago, hardened, and then slowly eroded away. The winds and rains and flash floods still work arranging and rearranging and, as in its neighboring park to the south, someday it will all change. Landscape Arch - that little six-foot section - will have worn away. Others will form and they, too, will dissolve until finally the tiny grains of sand, transported to distant places, will reassemble in some other shape and in some other time.

Geology dominates the landscape; it dominates life. There is little water and only sparse vegetation. Hardy junipers and pinyon pine grow in the bottomlands, seeking moisture wherever it can be found. The country is desolate and as inhospitable as any in the West.

Man has simply never been able to gain a foothold in canyon country - the white man that is. The Anasazi were here, and for probably a thousand years or so throughout all this land they hunted and farmed and made their pottery and baskets. How they survived we can only surmise; for their pictographs and petroglyphs, found all over the walls of Canyonlands, remain mute - intriguing and challenging, but mute. We don't even know, for example, why they left storehouses of corn, now dried stone-hard after a century of sun.

Butch Cassidy "hid out" here. Zane Grey wrote about it. John Wesley Powell put it on the map. But when it came to setting it aside as a national monument, there were those who thought "some people may be repelled and call the scenery ugly, not because it is drab or dull, but because it is so different as to be incomprehensible to them and therefore hostile".

"I cannot conceive of a more worthless and impracticable region than the one we now find ourselves in", wrote an early military explorer of the Canyonlands. He was searching for riches, and he found little of benefit in these canyons. Of course, he did not have a Geiger counter as did his twentieth-century counterpart, whose quest for uranium has left scars never to be erased. That was before 1964 and Canyonlands National Park.

But even in the park planning days, when the dedicated saw some 800 thousand acres of federally-owned land available, only 257 thousand were set aside. The governor of Utah "made it clear from the start" that he did not want park land to "lock up" resources, whatever they might be, and "damage his state's future economy."

Freeman Tilden, the grand old Philosopher who was adopted by the National Park Service in 1941 and at whose feet so many of us have sat – that marvelous thinker, who died in 1980 at the age of 96 – wrote in one of his most inspirational moments:

"I think America will have come to maturity when it will be possible to erect somewhere - probably it will be west of the Mississippi - a great bronze marker which will read:

Beneath these lands which surround you there lies enormous mineral wealth. However, it is the judgement of the American people, who locked up this area, that these lands shall not be disturbed, because we wish posterity to know that somewhere in our country, in gratitude to nature, there was at least one material resource that we could let alone."

Capitol Reef National Park

The colors are such as no pigments can portray. They are deep, rich and variegated; and so luminous are they, that the light seems to flow or shine out of the rock rather than to be reflected from it.

Geologist C. E. Dutton, 1880

Capitol Reef is one of the least known of our national parks. Perhaps it hasn't had the right press or an association with the right person to gain its place in the sun. Lincoln's address at Gettysburg, and later, Eisenhower's farm nearby, has always given that Civil War battle site in Pennsylvania just the right amount of exposure to overshadow other equally important historic sites. Capitol Reef had John C. Fremont and Butch Cassidy and a sprinkling of Indians, but never "front page stuff". Actually, in area Capitol Reef is larger than Bryce and Zion National Parks together, and in its own way is just as spectacular, but unlike its neighboring parks in Utah, Capitol Reef is off the beaten track and still remote as tourist attractions go.

Reading the geological story of Southern Utah and Northern Arizona is like looking down on the area as you fly from the East to California. It's all a little confusing and rings of a sameness: great upheavals and tiltings and depositions and erosions. One air passenger recently remarked, "They're all alike. If you've seen one, you've seen them all."

Not true! Still a bit confusing, perhaps, but each of these disruptions in the earth's surface is unique in its own way, not the least of which is Capitol Reef.

Actually the name is somewhat deceiving. This is not a reef and "capitol" refers to several dome-like formations. The origin of "reef," as it applies here, is really not known. Apparently it was an early geological term, perhaps from the nautical "reef" meaning barrier. At any rate, a barrier it was to the early explorers and pioneers, for the Waterpocket Fold, as this giant formation is known, runs about one hundred miles from Thousand Lake Mountain southeast to the Colorado River and can be crossed in only a few places.

The word "fold" is probably the best to use for a description of Capitol Reef. It was the most recent dramatic upheaval here and took place some sixty million years ago. Before that, say back 250 million years, the Capitol Reef geological story began with a shallow sea covering much of the Colorado Plateau. For the next nearly 200 million years this land heaved and sighed a dozen times, drawing and collecting waters that alternately laid down strata of new materials and eroded them away.

The great folding took place about the time the Rocky Mountains were uplifted to the east. All of the Colorado Plateau was raised a little in this process, but here in south-central Utah the earth's crust wrinkled into a long, S-shaped formation. There was other activity in the intervening years, and the evidence is here - boulders rounded from miles of rolling by water force, volcanic plugs from lava seeping into fissures - but for the most part it was eons of erosion that created this spectacular place. There seem to be no more cataclysmic upheavals in store for Capitol Reef but, as all across this land, the process of change is not finished. Melting snows, flash floods and torrential rains continue to wear and tear the landscape.

Exactly when and why Indians first came to the Capitol Reef area is unknown, but they were all over this canyon country, and here they left some of the best - and most mysterious - examples of their petroglyphs and pictographs.

This is canyon country, but it is also red country. The rock is red, in a dozen shades and tints and carved into an incredible display of pinnacles, towers and white, sandstone-capped domes, from which the park draws its name. And here and there, among the messages the Fremont Indians left behind, are scratched the names of pioneers who passed through - only their names to let us know they, too, had stopped for a moment in time.

Bryce Canyon National Park

Unka-timpe-wa-wince-pock-ich. Paiute for "Red rocks standing like men in a bowl-shaped canyon."

Bryce Canyon is changing. No, it's not disappearing; there's no need to rush. All our parks are changing in one fashion or another, such is the evolution of nature. Man has preserved them "in perpetuity," but at Bryce, where the rock formations are perhaps more delicate than at most others, the erosion is significantly pronounced. Protected forever from the ravages of the human, nature's processes continue. The towering pinnacles, those bright red and pink spires that have made Bryce Canyon so famous and popular, erode so easily and so rapidly that occasionally they crack and crumble or even collapse right before our eyes. In 1964 one of the favorite formations in the park, the arch at Oastler's Castle, collapsed, and one rock slide closed two of the "windows" outside the park, along the Zion-Mt. Carmel tunnel. Geologists predict that the rim of the Amphitheater is receding at the rate of one foot in 50 years.

Now before you run to the calculator, that means that if you are fortunate enough to spend five or six days there, the rim of the Amphitheater may be cut back about one two-hundredth of an inch. Hardly worth your time? Of course it is. Not to wait for a tumbling boulder or a slide of pebbles – it will be your lifetime, plus many others, before there is a change in the scenery – but the joy of Bryce Canyon is the breathtaking kaleidoscope of shapes and colors that dazzle the eye and mind.

The earliest white explorers and settlers who happened across much of our special scenery of the West were masters of the understatement. They were not poets or painters; these men and women did not come along until much later. They were trappers and traders and hunters and families seeking to carve out of these desolate places a bit of farm land, a plot of ground from which to draw a living. It is not so unusual, then, that their first revelations leave our generation, so fraught with show-business and political-type jargon, totally disappointed. Didn't they see what we see? To Ebenezer Bryce, Scottish emigrant and Mormon convert, who staked a claim and grazed his cattle here in the late 1870s, the canyon was simply "a hell of a place to lose a cow!"

Like his counterparts at Grand Canyon and Yosemite, Bryce found little pause in the spectacular, but he left his name behind. If he ever stood on the rim or walked the Indian trails beneath and saw any more than his cows, he never told us.

Bryce wasn't the first here, of course. There were Indians, though the evidence is thin and very little is known about them. We do know that Paiutes lived in the area in more recent times, for they left something of their impressions. As so frequently happened, the Indian was more poetic than the white man. For the spires in the amphitheater he gave us *unka-wa-wince-pock-ich,* "red rocks standing like men in a bowl-shaped canyon."

That statement rings of superstition, and no doubt its origins are in the legend that the Indians' ancestors were sinful folk who had defied the gods and were turned to stone. All of this seems to be supported by the lack of visible signs that Indians ever ventured among their "forebears".

The Spanish were in southern Utah in 1776, but it was the Mormons, nearly a century later, who first settled the Bryce area. Their pioneer communities sprang up all around this canyon, each digging some miraculous existence from the wilderness. It was probably not until sometime later than anyone really took stock in what Ebenezer Bryce had found.

It was nearly forty years before word began to trickle out. In 1916 an article appeared in a railroad magazine, and it wasn't long before tourists began to arrive. By 1923 the boundaries of Bryce Canyon National Monument had been set; it was doubled in size in 1928 and established as a national park.

Bryce Canyon is not really a canyon at all. Unlike nearby Zion, which is the canyon of the Virgin River, Bryce is the side of a plateau of varying kinds of stone that simply melted or washed away. Almost exclusively, water has been the erosive agent at Bryce; water in the form of heavy rains and snow and ice. It is more a washing process than a cutting or carving one as in the Grand Canyon.

There seems to have been some uplifting and tilting going on here in Utah millions of years ago, leaving great plateaus that form a natural staircase, so to speak, from Bryce southwest to the Grand Canyon. These plateaus, separated by the mighty forces of rivers, are all different in composition, and it is that composition, layer upon layer of sediment deposited when this land was all part of a great inland sea, that not only gave them their colors and names, but determined the erosion aftermath. There are the Chocolate Cliffs of Arizona at the Grand Canyon; working north are the Vermilion Cliffs, then the White Cliffs, the Gray Cliffs, and, at Bryce, the Pink Cliffs. The brilliant Pink Cliffs are about 60 million years old and about 8,000 feet above sea level. The Kaibab limestone of the Grand Canyon is 225 million years old and about 2,500 feet above sea level.

The rock formations in all of these great chasms are initially dependent on the kind of sediment laid down. Fresh water lakes covered the Bryce area, leaving a very fine-grained and soft siltstone and a slightly harder limestone. Sprinkled throughout are thin layers of shale. All of these erode at a different rate, thus the variety of shapes and sizes of formations.

What entices the eye most at Bryce Canyon is, of course, the color. Iron, in the form of iron oxides, mixed with varying concentrations of manganese and copper, is responsible. The more iron, the more pink and red; the more manganese and copper, the more lavender and green.

Bryce Canyon is really two parks: the high, forested plateau and the beautiful scenery below. While the shapes and colors of the forest are entrancing in themselves, it is the view below that captures the imagination. No photograph or book prepares you for what you see, but the names give you a hint. The first overlook, just inside the main park entrance, is called "Fairyland View". That almost says it all. "Tower Bridge," "Chinese Wall," Crescent Castle," "Sinking Ship," "Queen Victoria" – these are just a few of the intricate forms that set you off on what could be days of wandering in a fantasy land.

Someday the spires and arches will fall and the colors will change, but new ones will appear as the eroding waters seek their way to the seas: new domes and temples, some as delicate as needles, others as colossal as mountains, all molded by nature and untouched by human hand.

Zion National Park

A great reservoir of the serene order of nature.
Donald Culross Peattie

When man clashes with nature, he leaves his mark. His creativity and destruction stand for centuries and, while ultimately it may be subdued, it may never be erased. Each movement he makes is telling, and those who follow with instruments to measure this and that soon put together a story of human interference in the ways of nature.

There is one thing man leaves behind that in many ways is revealing and, irrespective of the intrusion, offers something the instruments can never detect. The mark he makes on a map or the name he gives a place or thing can often tell more of the powerful struggle, the emotions, the pain and sorrow, and the joys and ecstacies of his discoveries than any computer yet devised. Such is the case in the vast country of Zion National Park, where the Mormon pioneers, seeking their ecclesiastical haven,

found a certain peace and serenity. While their names, and those of others, for cliffs and domes and rugged canyons seem totally incongruous with the dramatic and massive forces of nature that created this place, the names stuck, and today we cannot help but agree with these people who articulated a vision. Zion itself means "the heavenly city of God." "Angels Landing" and the "Great White Throne" at first glance look like anything but something God would have sanctioned, but this is what they saw, and who are we to dispute these temples, altars, and pulpits?

Zion is a land of "peace and comfort," as they said, but to the solely geological eye, it takes some time to piece together this handiwork of nature and find that kind of solitude. The past was less than harmonious. The elements clashed with the earth, as indeed they do still. Monolith after monolith in this park stands as mute testimony to millions of years of erosion typical of southern Utah: fierce rivers and winds that wore away sandstone during the age of dinosaurs – and since.

Jedediah Smith, intrepid explorer and trapper, named the river that cuts through this canyon at Zion after his friend and contemporary, Thomas Virgin. It is the Virgin, which has its origins near Bryce Canyon and joins the Colorado at Lake Mead, that has ground out much of this semi-desert wilderness. Placid at times, it can rage during replenishing torrential rains, and when it does, its force against rock is incredible; three million tons a year is moved out of Zion and on to the Colorado.

One of the Virgin's tributaries, Pine Creek, is a potent example of what has happened at Zion. When the Zion-Mt. Carmel Road was tunneled through Bridge Mountain, six windows were cut into the mountain face for view-points along the highway. The debris - one can imagine the tons of rock - was thrown into Pine Creek basin below. Within a few months flash floods from summer rains roared through Pine Creek with mighty force and completely ground the rubble and carried it on downstream. One wonders how much of this man-made Lake Mead can handle before that body of water becomes a shallow pond. No one seems to be worried!

Zion's architecture is Navajo sandstone: sand dunes built on a desert plain for millions of years, slowly cemented in layers below sea level, and then raised, washed and crumbled away. The colors are nothing short of a pageant, all tints and shades of red, changing with the light, seldom the same from moment to moment.

Indians lived here too, as in Canyonlands, Arches, and all the other marvelous Utah and Arizona parks, but their time had passed long before Joseph Black, Mormon pioneer, settled along the canyon's outer edge.

John Wesley Powell, on his 1872 expedition, named the north fork of the Virgin canyon "Munkuntuweap" and the east fork canyon "Parunuweap," age-old Indian designations. But Joseph Black's vision prevailed. Zion became a national monument in 1909 and later, as its boundaries were expanded in 1937 and 1957, a national park.

Grand Canyon National Park

Though there are elsewhere deep canyons, some of even greater depth than the Grand Canyon ...there is not one that can match its vastness, its majesty, its ornate sculpture and its wealth of color. Whoever stands upon the brink of the Grand Canyon beholds a spectacle unrivalled on this earth.

Francois E. Matthes, *The Grand Canyon of the Colorado River*

A Texas cowboy grazing cattle in Arizona near the South Rim of the Grand Canyon suddenly found himself near the edge looking into that great chasm. He is reported to have removed his hat, wiped his brow, and said, "My God! Something has happened here!"

Hardly eloquent, that old cowhand, but search as you may for words at that first glimpse, most likely his will do. Nothing, not the camera, the canvas, or the poet, has prepared you for what may be the greatest visual shock man can experience: a pageant of time so huge and complex, so foreign to the senses, and yet so incredibly beautiful, that it is at once a frightening reality and an illusion.

J. B. Priestly wrote: "Those who have not seen it will not believe any possible description. Those who have seen it know it cannot be described."

It is best left unsaid. Preconceived notions vanish; the words of others prove inadequate; the camera fails. "My God! Something *has* happened here!"

This is not man's world. Unseen hands have created the most awesome spectacle on earth: a canyon 200 miles long, five to twelve miles wide, and 6,000 feet deep. The dimensions alone stagger the mind and, at first, turn you away. Yet, inevitably, you look back and gradually the magnificence of it all transcends that bewilderment and folds the human spirit into a glory of nature unknown before. This is the story of the earth itself, a geological calendar of time filled with the chaos of creation and the radiance of life going on. No one leaves unmoved.

When you suddenly come upon the Grand Canyon – and there is no other way, for that is the nature of the Colorado Plateau – you want to believe you are the first to see; you are the discoverer. Your eye searches and you compose; your mind sweeps the great rocks and cliffs, the gaiety of color, and soon you realize that in that brief moment it has all changed, and your words fly away. There are a thousand Grand Canyons as the sun moves across the sky, not a single minute the same as the one before. From the brilliance of sunrise, through dazzling sunsets, to the soft glow of the moon and stars, the Grand Canyon offers an infinity of moving experiences that mark the soul forever. And you are never the same.

Exploring the region in 1857, army Lieutenant Joseph Christmas Ives wrote: "It seems intended by nature that the Colorado River, along the greater portion of its lonely and majestic way, shall be forever unvisited and undisturbed." A man without vision – how wrong he was. He was not the first, of course. Indians had lived along the rim and in the canyon itself since the twelfth century; one tribe, the Havasupai, still farms a small oasis on the canyon floor. It was their ancestors who enticed Spanish explorers into the American Southwest. López de Cárdenas and the men of Coronado's expedition saw the canyon in 1540. But they, like Ives, were unimpressed. Searching for the legendary Indian cities of gold and silver, they found the canyon only a barrier in their path. It was left to a one-armed Civil War veteran, Major John Wesley Powell, to explore the Colorado River and bring the wonders of the Grand Canyon to the world. His journals are still fresh and vibrant and still used as guides along the river.

And, of course, Ives was wrong about visitors. In 1880 an ex-miner by the name of John Hance improved the old Indian trails into the canyon from the South Rim and began leading visitors down to the river. By 1901 there were hotels and camps, and within a few years a spur of the Santa Fe Railroad to bring the unbelievers. And with them came the entrepreneurs and the conservationists.

Efforts to preserve the canyon as a national park began in 1882, shortly after the establishment of Yellowstone, when Indiana Senator Benjamin Harrison introduced legislation in the Congress. It is hard to believe now, but the bill failed, and it was not until 1893, when Harrison became President, that he was able to protect even the forest abound the canyon from mining and timber prospectors. President Theodore Roosevelt in 1908 established the canyon as a national monument; by 1919 the Congress created the Grand Canyon National Park. But its dangers were not over. As late as 1965 there were threats to build two power dams on the Colorado River that would have flooded the canyon. One dam at Bridge Canyon would have backed the river into a reservoir, within the park. After a tough battle in the Congress, the Central Arizona Project was given approval in 1968, but without the dams, and the canyon was saved.

That's how I first saw the Grand Canyon – flooded – not with water but with clouds; a sea of clouds that had drifted in the night before and covered the abyss from rim to rim, a lake of white foam. This happens from time to time, but it could not have been a more perfect introduction. The sun was just coming up and so I perched on the stone wall behind the old El Tovar Hotel and waited. Slowly the mist burned off and there …I felt like the Texas cowboy. *What had happened here?*

Almost every day geologists learn something new about our planet from their studies in the Grand Canyon. For nearly a century now we have pieced together an astounding story of earth erosion and upheaval spanning two billion years of the earth's existence. A century of study, that's all. A drop in the bucket of time. All we really know is that it is the Colorado River, still flowing and still carving, that has changed this land. Beyond that, it is scientific theory that we see here, "nature's finest monument to the combined forces of uplift and erosion aided by an unlimited amount of time."

The Colorado begins in the Rocky Mountains and runs 1,450 miles to the Gulf of California. Along the way it is met by dozens of tributaries, the major of which is the Green River rising from the Wind River Mountains of Wyoming. In total, the Colorado and its tributaries drain a land area of 240,000 square miles, and it drops ten thousand feet over hundreds of rapids before it reaches the sea.

Once, before dams were built in its path, the Colorado ran untamed, carving its way through the canyon at a speed of two to twelve miles an hour. Today its force has been subdued, but still it moves more than a ton of silt each twenty four hours, and only after this is realized can one imagine what has transpired over the years.

During the high waters of 1927, more than twenty-seven million tons of suspended solids and dissolved materials were moved in one day. This is to say nothing of the rocks and boulders that are carried across the river bed.

Despite these impressive figures, the erosion is exceedingly slow. Since man has measured, it is estimated to be about six-and-one-half inches for each one thousand years. That's a lot of centuries just to "scratch the surface" so to speak.

But is has not been the Colorado alone that has created this spectacle. There were great land upheavals, tiltings caused by pressures from beneath the earth, which caused the river to run faster and erode deeper. As it did, the sides broke away and crumbled, only to be carried away by the rushing waters. Rain and melting snow caused further erosion, all the time cutting deeper and widening the gap.

And all of this goes on now right before our eyes. Our visits are so short, our time on earth such an infinitesimal moment on the geological calendar, that we will not see any great crumbling away, but barring new earth-building events, the Colorado will go on grinding and the walls of the canyon will continue to retreat until someday, millions of years from now, only a lazy river will meander across a plain where there was once this magnificent sight.

The future will be as awesome as the past, and we are only passing through as it all happens.

Mesa Verde National Park

It was 1280 – the year of the death of Kublai Khan, the great founder of the Mongol Empire on the other side of the earth from the Green Mesa. The people of the mesa knew nothing of Kublai Khan nor of the Mongols, though they could possibly have originated over there – sometime in the dim past perhaps having crossed the Aleutian bridge and found their way down to the tableland and canyon country where they now lived...
Freeman Tilden, *The National Parks*

On December 18, 1888, two cowboys, riding through the canyons and across the mesas of south- western Colorado looking for stray cattle, made one of the most important discoveries in North American archeology. One wishes that their motives had been less self-centered and the initial fruits of their find more scientific but, alas, like the beginnings of so many of our now protected historic areas in the United States, the story is not a pretty one.

Archeology had not come into its own as yet, but it was no deep, dark secret that early American man had established a civilization of sorts in the southwest many years before. Spanish explorers had found evidence in the 1600s, and cliff dwellings and remains of ancient campsites and villages ringed canyon walls and plateaus in the four corners area (Utah, Arizona, New Mexico, Colorado).

Richard Wetherill and Charles Mason were familiar with the Mancos Canyon country near the New Mexico border; Wetherill and his four brothers had established the Alamo Ranch near Mancos in 1879. This rugged land had already been charted by geological surveys, and Indian cliff dwellings were common sights near the ranch. But the most remarkable archeological ruins north of Mexico lay within their grasp, and for years eluded explorers and cowhands alike until that winter day in 1888.

Perhaps this is why the ruins of Mesa Verde remained untouched for so long. The land is forbidding to the traveler. Mesa Verde itself is an imposing escarpment rising 2,000 feet above the valley floor and 8,500 feet above sea level, the result of great prehistoric upheavals in the earth's crust. Even to the visitor today the approach to Mesa Verde is awesome. The huge plateaus above and to the south, however, are rich with the legacy of a lost, and, until Wetherill and Mason, forgotten culture, one of the most exciting of our national parks.

The two men who approached Cliff Palace that day were nothing short of good old American entrepreneurs. They saw the ruins for exactly what they were – a gold mine of ancient artifacts, and the following year they made their first large sale of pottery taken from Mesa Verde. Commercial exploitation continued until Mesa Verde National Park was established, and the Federal Antiquities Act was passed in 1906. Much was lost as the plundered artifacts scattered across the country to museums and private collections and, no doubt, some to destruction.

The ancient city is quiet now; only the wind whispering through the open windows and doorways of the cliff dwellings and the scampering of wild animals across its floors give it life. At one time, as early as 500 A.D., this was a thriving community of several thousand people, struggling to exist in an inhospitable land. That they made it work is remarkable, but evidence shows they had all of the makings of a successful agricultural society.

They were short, stocky, swarthy in complexion, with black hair, high cheek bones, and slightly-slanted, dark eyes, not unlike their ancestors and their descendants. No one knows how they spoke or communicated with each other; that they did, with considerable intellect, is quite evident. Their blending of agriculture, architecture and craftsmanship into a civilization of their own astounds modern man as he overlooks this unpretentious culture that somehow slipped away.

Mesa Verde, the "green table" in Spanish, is but a small part of the Colorado Plateau, the drainage basin of the Colorado River, typified by high mesas and deep canyons. Early Americans came here some ten thousand years ago, no doubt by the frozen Aleutian link to Asia. Today, man attempts to devise some pattern of life for this nomad. Although each little bone, bit of ash, and piece of carved stone offers a clue, the puzzle is still fragmented. Part lies in Mexico and Peru, part is scattered across the northern and eastern United States, and part lies here in this little corner of Colorado. To be sure, the Americans separated as they traveled south from Alaska. Some found a route farther south and established great civilizations. Some moved east and north and became the American Indian we know best and who survived the longest. Others moved to the sea and the southern California and Baja peninsula and barely existed. Those that stayed here seem to have remained for a period of about eight hundred years. Exactly why they left is the mystery that surrounds this place and has baffled archeologists for years.

That these cliff dwellers left, and left en masse, for other parts is a certainty. Their architecture suggests ample protection from human enemies, so that warring tribes were responsible seems remote. They were excellent farmers, however, and a long drought – narrow tree rings about the thirteenth century indicate this – or perhaps an exhausted soil that simply would not yield further existence, drove them to greener lands. Whatever the reason, the quest for survival led them elsewhere. They left no message telling us where, but throughout the tribes of the southwest, it seems certain, there is the blood of the people who once lived here – perhaps among the Hopis and other Pueblo Indians of New Mexico.

Search as we may, clues to the exodus of these people elude us, but we do not lack evidence of their life here. Spruce Tree House, for example, has been marvelously preserved. There are 114 living rooms and eight ceremonial rooms to this apartment complex, and each has offered a tiny bit of information on how the people lived and worked and played. The reconstruction of this period of our history is remarkably complete, despite the many losses, and it can be seen in graphic detail in the park museum.

Like the Inca of Peru and the Maya of Mexico – and perhaps they were really all part of the same – this civilization has vanished, leaving behind tantalizing bits and pieces of a gigantic puzzle. Sometimes we feel it is all done and there is nothing more to learn, but an archeologist's brush may yet dust off a pottery chip or an animal bone or a ceremonial trinket that will put it all together. Until then, Mesa Verde must be regarded as sacred to our American heritage. Whether or not we descend from these people, this place is part of us.

Petrified Forest National Park

The Forest That Was is now again the Forest That Is. But how changed!
Freeman Tilden, *The National Parks*

Economics has always been a major factor in the preservation of America's natural resources. Now, more than ever, we see government funding not only affect acquisitions but also the management of preserved areas. In 1892, however, it may have been an economic slump that in some ways stopped the plundering of a major national monument.

In 1853, just a few years after Arizona's great petrified forest was reported, a German artist, Baldwin Möllhausen, accompanying a military expedition into the Southwest, published an account of what he found and, in so doing, may have opened the door for wholesale vandalism:

"We collected small specimens of all these various kinds of fossil trees, and regretted that as our means of transport were so small we had to content ourselves with fragments, which certainly showed the variety of pertification, but not the dimensions of the blocks. ...All the way we went we saw ...great heaps of petrifications gleaming with such splendid colors that we could not resist the temptation to alight repeatedly and break off a piece, now of crimson, now of golden yellow, and then another, glorious in many rainbow dyes."

By the 1880s, when the Atlantic and Pacific Railroad worked its way west through northern Arizona, the beauty and mysteries of trees turned to stone brought tourists by the wagonload; and out in the same wagons when they left went bits and pieces of the forest. Like Möllhausen, they "could not resist the temptation to alight repeatedly and break off a piece."

No one really knows what was lost during the next twenty or thirty years – no one really knows how much was there to begin with – but it was staggering. Tourists sought the colorful stone for its beauty, but, more alarmingly, businesses sprang up overnight for other reasons. One South Dakota rock-polishing company took out over 400 tons of petrified wood to make mantels, tabletops, and pedestals. The marble-like stone brought outlandish prices and, no doubt, some pieces still decorate Victorian houses across America. It says something of our earliest attitudes about Petrified Forest to have had one of the first descriptions written by George Kunz, gem specialist for Tiffany's of New York.

By the 1890s vandalism had reached alarming rates. Logs were being dynamited for crystals, and in 1896 the first stamp mill was erected to grind the logs for abrasives. Commercial exploitation threatened simply to wipe the whole thing off the face of the earth, vitually before we could determine why it was there in the first place.

Then, miraculously, the bottom dropped out of the abrasive market, so to speak, and the stamp mill never turned its first wheel. There was a respite, and the concerned set about their quest for protection of this natural wonder.

It was not until 1906 that Petrified Forest National Monument was created and it was fifty-six more years before it attained national park status. But for the moment, at least, the vandalism was arrested. It has never really stopped. What Möllhausen began 120 years ago; a "fragment" here, a "fragment" there, is now estimated to be about twelve tons a year: twelve tons of priceless national property taken out of the park by thoughtless visitors. What is there about this petrified wood that has made it so utterly and compellingly fascinating?

The 148 square miles of land that now forms Petrified Forest National Park is like a giant jewel box. The colors of the Painted Desert, a portion of which is in the park boundaries, are incredibly beautiful; the silica and iron and manganese oxides of the stone trees sparkle like gems. But there is more to it than all this. There is the mystery of what Freeman Tilden called "The Forest That Was," made all the more mysterious by the mere fact that, try as one may, the eye finds absolutely no clue to the once tropical jungle of lush, exotic vegetation, lakes and swamps, animal life unknown today, and abundant rainfall that once was here. This is the desert, and a desert it has been for millions of years. No clue at all. That is unless you look closely.

Strewn across this barren, forbidding landscape are trees – well, they look like trees. Occasionally one will have roots, and on some the bark appears to have been preserved. But they are no longer upright and they are stone; stone hard enough to scratch all but the toughest of metals. Once they were giant conifers, not unlike some that still grow in South America. There were ferns and cycads and dozens of other plants. The land was flat, probably at about sea level and, according to the Plate Tectonics theory, about 1,700 miles closer to the equator, and roaming around all this was a collection of giant amphibious reptiles. This was 225 million years ago in what geologists call the Late Triassic period of the Early Mesozoic era. All of these things are still there – the trees and ferns and animals – fossilized. The clues are in this geological graveyard if you look.

What happened? Not simple. It's as complex as the evolution of the Grand Canyon, Yosemite, or any of the other national parks. First, the trees did not fall here ...not precisely here. They were carried here by rivers and streams that also carried great loads of sand and mud from distant mountains. Layer upon layer of silt was piled on the trees.

Somewhere in this process great layers of volcanic ash covered everything. Water from the marshes, rich with silica from the ash, penetrated the tissues of the trees, cutting off the supply of oxygen, preventing decay, and forming various kinds of quartz crystals: thus a tree that still looks like a tree but is stone.

Some of these trees, scientists think, look exactly as they did when they fell, intact and up to 160 feet in length. Others are chips and pieces as though loggers had been hard at work with axe and saw. Still others are in splinters. Within the park they are grouped in six separate concentrations: Giant Logs, The Long Logs, Crystal Forest, Jasper Forest, Blue Mesa, and Black Forest.

Once it was thought the supply of petrified wood was limitless, there seemed to be so much of it. It was this vast amount that prompted so much of the vandalism. This is no longer true. Geologists are certain that as time goes on erosion will uncover other trees beneath this land, as surely it will change, but the purpose of the park is to preserve what is left of this place, now, where nature gives us another kind of glimpse into the creation of the earth.

Cutting a living from this harsh land is difficult now and was no less so a thousand years ago. But there were Indians here and they left behind word that they had tried and somehow succeeded. Their petroglyphs of birds, snakes, and antelopes adorn Newspaper Rock, a seemingly aimless message so far untranslated. Occasionally a tool fashioned from petrified wood is discovered near several long since abandoned structures. Archeological digs indicate some occupation from the Basketmaker to Pueblo periods.

At least early man seemed to find some constructive use for the ancient trees – hammerstones, points, axes, building materials. In more recent times it took the F.B.I. twenty years to track down a Phoenix man who persistently hauled away cart-loads of petrified wood to purvey to the public.

Michael Frome wrote: "I can take everything I need and want from here without removing a thing."

Carlsbad Cavern National Park

I enter upon this task with a feeling of temerity as I am wholly conscious of the feebleness of my efforts to convey in words the deep conflicting emotions, the feeling of fear and awe, and the desire for an inspired understanding of the Divine Creator's work that presents to the human eye such a complex aggregate of natural wonders in such a limited space.

Robert A. Holley, 1922

A room with a ceiling twenty-five stories high and a floor of fourteen football fields – that's the Big Room of Carlsbad Cavern, one of the largest underground galleries of all the explored caves in the world.

One would think that this, like the attractions at Mammoth Cave in Kentucky, would have immediately appeared on the tourists lists when discovered. Not exactly. We don't know precisely when the first southwestern cowhand came across this cave, but it was in the late 1800s, too early for "tourists." Besides, Carlsbad, New Mexico, was hardly on the well-beaten track. Stages went by headed for California, but the caverns had another attraction, and beauty or fascination with geology played little part in it.

This was known as the Bat Cave at first, and that's logical. One of the things that may have sparked the first explorers was the thousands and thousands of bats that, each day at sunset, came fluttering out of the entrance in search of food – perhaps millions of them, since it now seems impossible to take a count. Well, where there are bats in this number, there has to be nitrate-rich guano, and there was – some fifteen thousand years of deposits.

This was the attraction at Carlsbad Cavern: bat guano. Within the twenty years just prior to its establishment as a national monument in 1923, some 100 thousand tons of guano were removed and sold as agricultural fertilizer.

In those days there *was* one man who saw something more than commercially successful business. His name was Jim White, and it was Jim who, more than anyone, moved the Congress to protect this marvelous temple of underground geology. He had explored it and he preached its beauty with such passion that he became its first chief ranger.

Jim White wasn't the first to see the cavern. Early Indians did not document their visits, but someone of the Basketmaker period was there. He left behind a sandal. That may have been four thousand years ago.

Carlsbad Caverns' history goes back much farther in time, perhaps 200 million years, when those geologic forces and seas formed the nearby Guadalupe Mountains. Like in other underground yawnings, sediments were laid, bends and cracks occurred, waters dissolved the rock, creating water-filled cavities, the cavities drained, and mineral-laden water seeped into them to redeposit the rock as cave formations.

One wonders if all of these processes were as beautiful in the making as they appear today. It almost seems as if some divine decision was made purposely to seclude our geological marvels until man was ready to see and appreciate them. At any rate, it was millions of years in the making and the finished product, if indeed it is finished, carries a master's touch.

Carlsbad Cavern is beautiful. It is enormous and not yet completely explored. Seven miles of chambers and passageways are open; more exist that may lead into the Guadalupes – no one knows for certain. But those which one may visit are a wonderland of the weird. Almost ghostly when specially lighted, columns standing at every turn; better still, they loom from the floor. Overhead hang stalactites in the shape of intricate chandeliers or frozen waterfalls; one spectacular ceiling formation is called the "Sword of Damocles." The Green Lake Room, the King's Palace, the Queen's Chambers ...each little alcove and niche has its own special charm.

And the bat still flies. Despite the fantasyland deeper into the caverns, and the almost dread fear the little bat creates in us all, the nightly flight is one of the chief attractions here.

Would that we held this strange animal in more respect. Contrary to popular belief, this is not the vampire of fiction. Actually it is clean, timid, and a blessing in disguise. Those nightly forays into the countryside are to feed, and feed they do, on millions of beetles, moths, and other insects.

But, as time passes, the bat population, like so many other things with which man tampers, is affected. Hundreds of thousands are still there, and it is hoped that the population has now stabilised. But it is a diminished population. Outside, we are spreading pesticides to control the insects. One wonders...

Guadalupe Mountains National Park

Though appearing like a forbidding fortress, the Guadalupe range, like the nearby desert, has secrets it yields only to those wise enough to look for them and with time enough to explore.

John Barnett, former park naturalist,
Guadalupe Mountains National Park

Guadalupe Mountains National Park is everything that Texas is not supposed to be: a marine barrier reef, eight-thousand-foot mountains and, within the space of a few miles, a series of climate zones that range from Mexican desert to Canadian snows. It was a long time before anyone really saw or appreciated this somewhat bizarre scenery in southwest Texas. As a matter of fact, it seems that almost everyone who came near these mountains tried their best to ignore them. The very earliest Indian nomads passed through, perhaps as long as twelve thousand years ago, but evidence shows they did not tarry. Spanish explorers marching north from Mexico seemed totally unaware that the mountains existed. The first American maps of Texas charted the Guadalupes, but incorrectly, and U.S. Army survey teams consistently avoided them. It was not until 1849 that anyone took the time to acknowledge this "high range of mountains called the Sierra Guadalupes," but even then it was only in passing.

Then came John Bartlett, commissioner of the Mexican boundary survey in 1850. His was the first description that drew any public attention. Still it was another eight-or-so years before anyone other than the Apache Indian traveled these parts. In 1858 the Butterfield Overland Mail Stage began a short-lived run between St. Louis and San Francisco. Its route was just west of Guadalupe Pass. Few coaches got through without confronting Indian raids, however, and the line was soon abandoned. The Apache was master of the Guadalupes, and the white man's encroachment was not received well. Peace with the Indian came slowly and only by the persistence of the U.S. Cavalry.

At first glance, startled by the starkness of the landscape, one wonders why the mountains were not left to the Indians who somehow eked out a living here. Conditioned by Zane Grey and Hollywood, the imaginative mind sees bandits, cowboys and cattle rustlers, and if you look up above the canyon walls, it's not difficult to conjure a chief mounted on his pony gazing out over the desert floor. In fact, that was about the limit of the inhabitants here until the early 1900s. Billy the Kid was known to hide out here, and the old Chisholm Ranch and the Lincoln County War are legendary names in these parts.

It is doubtful that any of the men of the desert knew or cared about the make-up of the Guadalupes. No one did until the geologists arrived, and then, much to everyone's surprise, they found the top of these mountains to be the world's most extensive fossil organic reef. Such a phenomenon seems totally incongruous to Texas. There is no sea, no marine life, nothing with which to relate. Yet there was once, here in southwest Texas and southeast New Mexico, some 250 million years ago in the Permian period, a shallow, saltwater inland ocean. It had settled in an area that today might be bordered on the north by U.S. 82, on the east by Texas 18, the south by U.S. 67 and 90, and the west by Texas 54. That's stretching it a bit, but the outer perimeter of the sea can be traced by this great barrier reef in a circle of New Mexico and Texas mountains: the Guadalupes, Apache, Glass, and Sierra Diablo. Much of the reef is buried beneath the earth, but here at Guadalupe Mountains National Park it is evident in the highest peaks in Texas.

Near the edge of this inland sea, in shallow water, lived lime-secreting algae that over eons of time built a reef not unlike that found off the coast of Queensland, Australia. As the water supply to the sea ceased to flow, the basin became stagnant and evaporated, leaving great salt flats. But the reef had been built, and despite the upheavals and cracks that occured in the earth in subsequent years, the reef remained.

Should the eye concentrate solely on the mountains, fascinating in themselves with their fossils and ancient limestone deposits, the vast ecological range of the park will be missed. Four distinct climate zones and three ecologic zones separate the basin floor from Guadalupe peak; climates ranging from that of northern Mexico to southern Canada. Cactuses and drought-resistant shrubs populate the desert-like floor, while the upper canyons and highlands are covered with ponderosa and limber pines and aspen. This wide divergence of environments has resulted in a profusion of animal life that, fortunately for all, has enjoyed nearly total protection for the past fifty years: elk, deer, bear, mountain lion, bighorn sheep, and some 200 species of birds.

Guadalupe Mountains National Park was established in 1972, for the most part through the generosity and foresight of two men who lived in and loved the mountains and who, rather simply put, wanted to see the land preserved. In 1961 Wallace Pratt, an aging oil executive who had bought a large portion of McKittrick Canyon in the Guadalupes, gave 5,632 acres to the United States. "I had been told ...that it was the most beautiful spot in Texas," Pratt said. "So I drove a hundred-odd miles [in 1921] in an old Model T to see for myself." In 1961 Pratt found that he could no longer care for his ranch which, even then, was called "a masterpiece of conservation and preservation." "We thought, 'My God, what's going to become of this,'" he said. "We thought somebody ought to take care of this wonderful barrier reef, protect it..."

A few years later another "specimen" property adjoining Pratt's became available and the national park was born. J.C. Hunter of Abilene, Texas, owned more than 70,000 acres, some 120 square miles of the Guadalupe Mountain range. For years the Hunter family had raised angora goats and had established a profitable business in mohair wool. But the Hunters had a healthy respect for the land which, like the Pratt ranch, was in pristine condition. Hunter asked $1,500,000. It was a bargain.

Guadalupe Mountains National Park is an extraordinary land, its interrelated geology and ecology delicately balanced, but because two men and their families cared, it has been preserved.

Big Bend National Park

Nowhere have I found such a wildly weird country. Never have I beheld such a display of glory as falls at sunset on the bald head of the Chisos Mountains.
William Ferguson, 1895

Some day, far into the future, archeologists roaming the desert canyons of the Big Bend country will happen across the fossil remains of a North African camel and ponder how it got there. Recorded history will tell and the archeologists will note the anachronism as another in a long list of contradictions. This is a land of contradictions and contrasts.

Nestled in the arid, rugged, and forbidding great curve of the Rio Grande in southwest Texas, Big Bend country is a lesson in true solitude, where man meets the conflicting forces of nature and wonders how anyone, anything, has survived. This is a land of incredible heat and freezing cold, virtually without rainfall, yet blooming with life, a land of high mountains and basins, great distances and microscopic life, gentle beauty amid desolate surroundings, brooding silences and the lilting song of a wren. It is all this and much more; endless space, endless time on the horizons of America's frontier.

For one hundred miles along the southern boundary of Big Bend National Park – and the border between the United States and Mexico – the Rio Grande winds its way first southeast and then abruptly northeast, still carving, as it has done for eons, through desert and mountain. This is harsh country, where Texas ranchers once called eighty thousand acres of pasture land with two mules over-stocked. Yet there is a singular beauty that satisfies even the visitor who sports Yellowstone and Yosemite bumper stickers.

The geology of Big Bend is complex, but the Indian has a simple explanation: when the Great Creator had finished building the earth and the sky and the stars, he had a huge pile of stony rubble left over. He gave it a toss towards the Rio Grande and it all landed here ...at Big Bend.

Would that it were that easy to understand. Like much of southwest Texas, Big Bend country was under shallow seas millions of years ago. As the continent heaved this way and that, some of this land was exposed and great swamps grew, harboring dinosaurs and huge, winged reptiles. And then the continent shifted again, this time pushing up the Rockies and the Sierra Madres. Here the Chisos Mountains sprang up between the two. Thousands of years later the Rio Grande began to carve its way through this mass of twisted rock. Now it seems to be the only living thing to have survived.

Big Bend is desert: *despoblado*, the Spanish called it, uninhabited land. It occupies part of the vast Chihuahuan Desert that covers much of northern Mexico and southern Texas. *Chisos* expresses its mood. Loosely translated, Chisos means "ghost" or "spirit,"

although modern linguists suggest it is derived from the Castilian *hechizos*, meaning "enchantment". It is all that.

It takes little imagination to see Spanish conquistadors, Apache and Comanche warriors, bandits and marauders making their way across the desert floor. Their shadows blend into a composite, romantic mirage of the past in this rather overwhelming country where there is little grace or charm, and beauty is a word too soft for these harsh and forbidding sights.

Despite its hostile nature, history has not passed Big Bend. Early cave-dwelling Indians left their pictographs; but the Spanish, seeking golden cities to the north in the sixteenth century, avoided it. The Apache and Comanche in the mid-1700s used it as a stronghold and last bastion for survival. By the late-nineteenth century the white man, mostly in the uniform of the United States Army, had entered and firmly established command. With the exception of 1916, when there was a brief flourish of Mexican arms from across the border, and Big Bend country has been quiet since.

This history is the West at its wildest and bears the imprint of the most notorious of outlaws and gunmen who rode through the frontiers. To say they built or won the West is hardly fair to the settlers who fought to tame the land. But the Chisos Mountains that sheltered them, and the desert that provided them battleground, are as much a part of our heritage as any house on the prairie.

"You can see forever," a friend has said. The Chisos are the southern-most mountains in the United States, rising over six thousand feet, the highest peak 7,835 feet above sea level. The desert sprawls below – Texas to the north, Mexico to the south – and you can see well into both. And dividing it all is the Rio Grande, the Great River. This is true wilderness, where once roamed fifty-foot crocodiles, and in their steps the Indians and cowboys and western pioneers, and now people of all walks of life.

Big Bend became a national park in 1944 with the help of the Texas Legislature, but tame it ...no one can. There's no need to. Bring it back to life ...perhaps; livestock grazing stripped it of its sparse vegetation. The plants, over one thousand species, are coming back, and there are 400 species of birds recorded. The desert teems with wildlife. If you look hard enough you can see mountain lion, javelina, snakes, turtles, tarantulas, and...

Oh! Yes. The camel. The great camel experiment. In 1856 Secretary of War Jefferson Davis – he later became president of the Confederacy – imported eighty camels from the Middle East for transportation in the West. It made sense. This was desert; the camel came from the desert. For a while it worked, but after the Civil War the experiement failed. Railroads pushed west and, to be very honest about it, the camel simply never overcame the "political pull" of the old, faithful Missouri mule. What was left of the herd was turned loose to roam free. Now and again their traces are found – just another small chapter in the Big Bend story.

Glacier National Park

Give a month at least to this precious reserve. The time will not be taken from the sum of your life. Instead of shortening, it will indefinitely lengthen it and make you truly immortal.
John Muir

John Muir could have been writing about any of America's national parks, but Glacier is a very special place – some claim the most beautiful of all the parks – and it takes time to enjoy and understand, time never missed in the scheme of things. There's an old story told – told by nearly everyone who writes about Glacier, but well worth repeating – of the man who seemed disappointed that there was "nothing exciting" to do at the park. What the hell do you expect me to do here," he asked, "look at the *scenery*?"

It is quite difficult to believe that anyone can enter Glacier and not be in awe of the mighty works of nature. Assuming that some fail to see, one can only feel sorry for those who seek more exciting things than "a look at the scenery." The towering majesty of Glacier National Park is as spectacular as any place on earth and to see is to communicate with nature. Here is truly a wonder of America, indeed of the world.

The grandeur is not all ours. We share it with Canada, where the northern extension of the Livingston Range in Alberta is Waterton Lakes National Park. Together the two form the Waterton-Glacier International Peace Park, authorized and established in 1932 by the United States Congress and the Canadian Parliament as "a symbol of permanent peace and friendship."

The mountains of Glacier National Park are a part of the Rockies, that upheaval of mountain building that began about 75 billion years ago and extended in distance from South America through Mexico and the United States and Canada into Alaska and the Aleutians. But what we see here is much more than just mountain building; it is mountain shaping in the classical sense. The park is named for the prehistoric forces that formed it; the mighty glaciers of the ancient ice ages. And there are fifty-some within the park that still press down the mountain slopes, grinding and carving and shaping as their predecessors did eons ago.

Of course, the mountains came first. Geologists vary in their estimates of exactly when, but it makes little difference. They *are* in agreement, however, on how it all happened. After millions of years of sediment deposits, as much as thirty-five thousand feet, from a shallow body of water that covered the western United States, this land began to warp and buckle and crack, and ancient rock pushed up and through the earth's crust. Unlike the Southern, or Colorado Rockies – rather orderly they – this three hundred mile range was squeezed together in a vise-like grip that forced the rock sideways to the east in a fold called an overthrust. The geological formations that are evident in Glacier's mountains, and attract scientists from the world over, show that this mass was pushed some forty miles eastward. The mountains approached from the east give the impression that they were pushed up right where they are. There are no foothills similar to those on the western slopes. The farthest extension of this overthrust is Chief Mountain in the northeast corner of the park. Here the younger and older rock, one having overlapped the other, are quite evident.

But all the mountains here have been worn away and shaped by the ice ages that once covered all but the very peaks. There were four great periods of ice that worked their way through these mountains, the first beginning some three million years ago, the last about ten to twelve thousand years ago. It was these great rivers of ice flowing around the mountains that created the "Matterhorn" peaks.

The glaciers in the park today, like Blackfoot, Grinnell and Sperry, are examples of what was here before. These have come only recently in time, perhaps as late as a thousand years ago, and they too are rapidly melting away. When first discovered in the late 1800s, both the Grinnell and Sperry glaciers covered areas of one thousand acres. Today they are each only about three hundred acres in size. On a much smaller scale, these glaciers are doing what the others did.

At the height of the glacial periods, these valleys were filled with ice, as much as three thousand feet thick, and at least one extended forty miles into the Montana plains. The glaciers' paths can be measured by the knife-like ridges, the peaks, the passes, the valleys, and the debris left behind. Some flowed quite rapidly, that is rapidly for a glacier – several feet a day. Today's ice flows much more slowly; Grinnell has been "clocked" at about one inch a day. Nonetheless, the constant motion of the thick, plastic-like ice at the bottom, combined with the huge boulders and rocks it carries, is what has sliced the mountains and dug the valleys and basins.

Glacier is one of the few areas south of the Canadian border with a subarctic climate, and the plant and animal life reflects that. But despite the deceptive, barren-like appearance of the mountains, the park is a true wilderness, an ideal setting for a wide variety of wildlife and plants.

The mountain heights capture the abundant rainfall from the Pacific coast on the western slopes, producing dense forests of larch, spruce, fir and lodgepole pine. Here the western red cedar and hemlock reach their eastern boundaries. On the east side, where the Montana plains and the mountains meet rather abruptly, the prairie flora prevails: pasque flower, red and white geraniums, gailardia, asters, shooting star, and the Indian paintbrush. The short-lived alpine display is every bit as splendid and can be easily seen along the hundreds of miles of trails through the upper reaches of the park.

One of the joys of Glacier National Park is that the wildlife, once hunted for sport and food, is now protected. If there is such a thing as animals sensing their freedom, it is probably demonstrated best here. While the deer, elk, moose and bear are no more friendly here than in other parks, they are abundant and for the most part visible to the visitor. If you are "looking at the scenery," seldom will you have to complain about sightings.

Man confers "official" on many things. Here he has given the distinction to the mountain goat, the "official" animal of Glacier National Park. Unpretentiously, this mammal wears its title well. Actually it is an antelope and not a goat at all, but seen scampering along the most precipitous cliffs and slickest rock formations, titles and names matter little to it or the visitor. It is a marvelous animal that astounds you and at the same time makes you envious of its agility.

Peter Fidler, a scout for the Hudson's Bay Company in 1792, was the first white man to see the Waterton-Glacier area. He found the Piegan Indian had been here long before and, no doubt, other prehistoric Indians prior to that. Settlement was slow and tedious through the nineteenth century as rugged terrain and fierce Indian reluctance to yield territory presented barriers. The conquering of the Indian was much as in other areas of the West, and ultimately the pressures of the fur trade and mining interests forced a withdrawal, and the "dudes" from the East moved in.

The Great Northern Railroad is as responsible as anything for the development of Glacier National Park. By 1891 it had laid a line across Montana and over Marias Pass to Kalispell, along the southern end of the area. Within thirty years of the railroad coming, the previously envisioned mining potential decreased dramatically. The Great Northern, politicians, and conservationists joined hands in urging the Congress to preserve the area in its natural state. Glacier became a national park on May 11, 1910.

Nowhere is the work of glaciers quite so evident as here in Montana, a place of extraordinary beauty. It has been called the "Crown of the Continent," where the mountains unfold into a panorama of cathedral-like spires before the eyes. It was meant to be seen, to be felt, to be worshipped.

Yellowstone National Park

It is like the creation of the very devil himself: angry forces of the underworld locked in combat beneath the earth with the sounds and visible fury of their struggle seeping through fissures to enthrall the curious above ground who come to see what the forces of fire and ice have spawned.
Stewart L. Udall, *The National Parks of America*

H. Allen Smith, in his marvelously funny book, *The Compleat Practical Joker,* tells the story of two Eastern college boys who worked as summer-seasonal employees at Yellowstone National Park. Both had consistent run-ins with a cantankerous, and somewhat pompous, old ranger whose duty it was to guide visitors to Old Faithful. Bent on getting even after a fretful summer, the boys plotted. Their opportunity came on the day before they left for home.

Several times a day the ranger would lead his group of attentive tourists to the famed geyser, lecturing as he went about the wonders of nature's great underground pressures that caused Old Faithful to erupt like clockwork. He would look at his watch and carefully time his words so that, on cue, he could dramatically sweep his arm toward the geyser just as it grandly spouted into the air.

The night before their last day, the young seasonals went to a junkyard in West Yellowstone and bought an old automobile steering wheel and column, several plumber's pressure gauges, and an assortment of pipes and elbows. The next day, just off to the side of Old Faithful, in view of the visitors but out of sight of the ranger when he turned to address his audience, the boys set up their equipment: the steering column in the ground with the gauges and pipes placed strategically by its side. They waited.

Soon the little guided troop made its way to the spot, and the ranger turned to deliver his curtain-raising speech. The boys busied themselves tapping pipes and checking gauges as the ranger explained how at that very moment the natural pressures were building beneath them and how – he looked at his watch – in just a few seconds Old Faithful would blow. Just as he swung his arm and pointed, one of the boys yelled, "Let 'er go, Charlie!" The other gave the steering wheel a vigorous spin ...and Old Faithful shot a hundred and fifty feet into the air.

God forbid ...to this day there may be people convinced that Yellowstone National Park is a complete fraud and that Old Faithful is run by an elaborate, man-made, underground steam system.

Well, there is a steam system under Yellowstone, not man-made, but a steam system known the world over and one which has gained particular attention recently in these energy-conscious times. As if there are not enough threats to Yellowstone – acid rain, air pollution, visitor impact – one trembles at the thought of real gauges, pipes, and steering wheel-type valves controlling geothermal power. The two young college lads may well have been more prophetic than they ever thought.

This is where it all began: Yellowstone, the first wilderness set aside as a national park. Yosemite supporters will argue this, and with some credibility. Yosemite Valley was given <u>state</u> park status in 1864, but it all belonged to California for twenty-six years before it was entrusted to the federal government. Yellowstone National Park was established by an act of Congress in 1872. The timing and "who's on first" dialogue is so totally irrelevant today that it has been relegated to little more than friendly barbs between park rangers.

There has always been something special about the Yellowstone country, but its earliest native inhabitants seemed hardly awed by the spectacular scenery and the earth's peculiar palpitations. "There is frequently heard a loud noise like thunder, which makes the earth tremble," they said and, according to an early explorer, "they state that they seldom go there because their children cannot sleep – and conceive it possessed of spirits, who were adverse that men should be near them." The Crow, Blackfeet, Northern Shoshoni, and Bannock all lived around the region and hunted through what is now the park – certainly their ancestors did, perhaps as much as five to ten thousand years before – but when the first Europeans came in search of furs, they found only a "timid and impoverished" band of the Shoshoni, known as "Sheepeaters," who had made a home here.

The white man seems to have skirted the Yellowstone plateau in his early travels west; the Lewis and Clark expedition came close in 1804. John Colter, a member of that expedition, broke away on the return east and became the first known white man to see the wonders of what we now define as the park. He never wrote about it but he talked a great deal and, while at first many of his stories were discounted as exaggerations and just plain untruths, his name was left behind here just as it was in the Grand Tetons.

The fur trade and reports of gold brought many Easterners into the country. but, like the words of John Colter, their tales of boiling springs, geysers, mountains of glass, and other phenomena were given little credence. The editor of *Lippincott's Magazine* rejected one story with: "Thank you, but we do not print fiction." When another magazine carried a Yellowstone article, a reviewer wrote that the author "must be the champion liar of the Northwest." And so Mi-tsi-a-da-zi, "the land of Rock Yellow Water," as the Sioux called it, remained little known to the public and something of a mystery. Trappers and hunters continued to come, and the "tall tales" lured the curious, but even the most eloquent journals were not convincing. The public wanted some proof, something official, and it came in 1870 in the day-by-day report of a young cavalry lieutenant, Gustavus

Doane, who accompanied Henry Washburn, surveyor-general of the Montana Territory, to "the falls and lakes of Yellowstone."

Doane was neither geologist nor writer, but he had a keen eye and a gift for description. He climbed what is now Mount Washburn, and he measured the height of geysers, and he tried to describe what had happened here. "A single glance at the interior slopes of the ranges," he wrote, "shows that a former complete connection existed, and that the great basin has been formerly one vast crater of a now extinct volcano. The nature of the rocks, the steepness and outline of the interior walls, together with other peculiarities, render this conclusion a certainty." Doane was very nearly right, and his report became a classic.

It was one of those rare periods in history, perhaps unique to America, when things seemed to fall into the right place. About this time the first back-to-nature movement was beginning; Thoreau's and Emerson's essays were being read, and conservationists were calling for preservation of the natural state of things. Thoreau had written: "Why should not we …have our national preserves …in which the bear and panther and even some of the hunter race may still exist and not be 'civilized off the face of the earth' …for inspiration and our true re-creation? Or should we, like villains, grub them all up for poaching on our own national domains?"

Washburn's expedition had consisted of some rather prominent people, and it led to the march on Congress. Yellowstone, as yet untouched by those who would exploit the land, must be saved. The idea had been discussed while yet in the wilderness. "It was at the first camp after leaving the Lower Geyser Basin," wrote Cornelius Hedges, a lawyer and correspondent, "when all were speculating which point in the region we had been through would become most notable, when I first suggested uniting all our efforts to get it made a national park, little dreaming such a thing was possible.

It was probably the worst possible time for such a proposal in terms of government stability and finance. The country, rocked by the Civil War and still in the throes of westward expansion, faced the harsher realities of life. To quote Freeman Tilden: "It was still a pioneer country, except for the selvage along the Eastern seaboard, and words like *aesthetics, natural beauty,* and *spiritual values* were received with a squint. Man must eat; man must thrive; spiritual values should be left for posterity. It was all quite natural. The unnatural thing was that such idealism prevailed." Yellowstone National Park was established March 1, 1872.

Fortunately for all, the creation of Yellowstone as a preserve came before western land exploitation made its way into this high country, so we can only speculate what might have happened given another century. We know the wildlife was already endangered from hunting and trapping and remained so for a number of years after the park was formed. In fact some species were nearly destroyed from the mere lack of law enforcement. If gold had been discovered – and certainly it was sought – politics would have been a formidable force with which to reckon. As it was, during the early years there were plenty of second thoughts about the two million acres set aside "as a public park or pleasuring-ground for the benefit and enjoyment of the people." Pressures on the Congress were enormous: the timber, railroad, and cattle industries, to say nothing of those interested in mineral

rights, and even the military, who claimed the Indian would never be subdued until his primary food souce, the buffalo, was destroyed. The Congress wavered as individual members urged the government to get out of the tourist business and the raising of wild animals.

Only those who take time to see this park – and understand what they see – can appreciate the bargain Washburn and the others got for their time and trouble in 1870-72. Yellowstone National Park is nearly 3,500 square miles of virgin wilderness; land unchanged except by nature itself. Little of the total area has been affected by man's intrusion. Not only is it one of the nation's largest wildlife preserves, it is a geologic wonderland unlike any on earth: spouting geysers, bubbling mudpots, steaming fumaroles and pools of boiling water, hundreds of ponds and lakes surrounded by dense forests, rivers and streams rushing through black and yellow canyons, eight-thousand-foot plateaus, and ten-thousand-foot mountains; and populated throughout by bear, moose, elk, bison, deer, antelope, dozens of other mammals and hundreds of species of birds.

If we were to place an age on this land, it would be over 2.7 billion years; that's the age of the most ancient rock. But rather than repeat the story of the Rocky Mountain building, of which this is basically a part, it is more important to come forward to about 600 thousand years ago, when the last of three great volcanic eruptions took place. That was right here, and the caldera or crater that formed is the Yellowstone basin. This chain of events has been estimated to be of mammoth proportions, unlike any in recorded times. Huge quantities of extremely hat ash were thrown out onto the land. It must have been like all the geysers, mudpots, thermal pools, the earthquakes – yes, there are tremors of some sort every day – all of this happening at once on a scale a million times greater and for a long period of time. There are no adjectives to describe it all.

Then all was quiet …all but the pot simmering just beneath the surface. It simmers still …and you can see it, hear it, smell it. Is it the age-old activity still dying away, or is it a renewal, or perhaps the birth, of some new fury that will one day, once more, alter this landscape?

For those who may have been taken in by the pranksters, there are no valves or gauges or pipes. Let's trust there may never be. If Yellowstone is to be disturbed, it will be at the hands of nature …in its own good time.

Rocky Mountain National Park

Room – glorious room, room in which to find ourselves.
Enos Mills

Plodding their way across the Central Plains toward the Western lands they had only heard about, nineteenth-century American pioneers were completely unprepared for the barrier that stood in their way. They were already a mile high in altitude, but had so gradually and imperceptibly traveled that they were shocked at this giant wall looming up from the flat tableland as though a dark curtain had dropped from the sky. They were only vaguely aware of the Rockies, if indeed they had ever heard of them. To many, these mountains would be their undoing; to others, the barrier would be but an introduction to the West and the hardships that lay ahead.

While travel today is much more comfortable and we know that the front range of the Rockies awaits, the first sight is still as awesome as it must have been to those early pilgrims in covered wagons. From many miles east of Denver a certain sense of drama fills the air as the straight horizon takes on a slightly jagged line which slowly becomes pyramids in the sky. By the old gold rush town of Denver the Rockies have fulfilled their promise of one of the greatest mountain masses in the world.

The Rockies are a part of a much larger system of mountains in the western hemisphere: the cordillera (Spanish, meaning chain of mountains), as it is called, which extends from Argentina to Alaska. In North America this vast crustal disturbance is divided into sections: the Rockies, the Plateaus, the Basins and Ranges, the Sierra Nevada, the Cascades, and the Coast ranges. Within its own family these are the Southern or Colorado Rockies. The range in Wyoming is the Middle Rockies, in Idaho and Montana the Northern Rockies, and in Canada the Canadian Rockies.

At the center of the Southern Rockies is Rocky Mountain National Park, no less than 105 peaks rising above 10,000 feet, more than 400 square miles of virtually unspoiled nature and scenic splendor set aside by the federal government in 1915. It was a long time in preparing: some 300 million years, in fact, when the ancestral mountains began uplifting from the seas that covered the western United States. About 70 million years ago the last inland ocean drained away. This was the beginning of what we see now. For the next 60 to 65 million years there were alternating periods of volcanic activity, uplifting, and erosion. Then, some seven million years ago, there was a final broad uplift of the region. The great ice ages - several of them - followed, and glaciers cut and shaped the Rocky Mountains we know.

Man saw none of this, although geologists believe that several of the small glaciers here now may date back to a minor ice age of some 800 years ago. As in Grand Teton, Glacier, and Yellowstone National Parks, where some evidence remains, there may have been ancient hunters in these mountains as early as 10,000 years ago - probably the ancestors of the Arapahoes and Utes found here in the nineteenth century. But these mountains played little role in the winning of the West. Their human history prior to the nineteenth century is sparse.

Lieutenant Zebulon Pike, for whom Pike's Peak is named, came to the mountains in 1806, and Colonel S. H. Long, who gave his name to the highest point in the park, led a party to the foot of the mountains in 1820. But it was not until 1860 that the first family settled here. Joel Estes built a cabin in what is now Estes Park, just outside the main entrance to Rocky Mountain National Park. He stayed for only six years, selling his property for, some say, a team of oxen.

The 1850s gold rush that built Denver never really affected the mountains. The Irish Earl of Dunraven selected 15,000 acres of land as a private hunting preserve in the 1870s, but by 1906 it was all sold, some to F.O. Stanley, the man who built the famed Stanley Steamer automobile and the grand Stanley Hotel that since 1909 has served tourists in Estes Park.

Then came the man who was most directly responsible for the establishment of the national park. Enos Mills came here in 1884 at the age of 14. Self-educated and a hard worker, Mills became one of America's leading naturalists. Often called the "John Muir of the Rockies," he met Muir and they developed a lifelong friendship. Around 1900 Mills began publishing books and articles on the Rockies. For seven years he worked at his own expense to create a national park here, and he lived to see the dedication ceremonies on September 4, 1915. Ironically, he died in 1922 of blood poisoning – his debilitated condition aggravated as the result of a subway accident – in New York City, far from his beloved land.

This is winter land and summer land. The Rockies are to be enjoyed year-round. "Room in which to find ourselves," Mills said. A glorious room filled with wildlife - the great American elk, mule deer, black bear, cougar, coyote, the bighorn sheep - the haunting tundra with its precious, tiny wildflowers that cling so helplessly for their few weeks of life; the streams and forests - all of this in infinite variety. A place to find ourselves.

Facing page: vast, limestone cliffs tower over the Rio Grande at the mouth of Santa Elena Canyon in Big Bend National Park, southwest Texas.

Facing page: (top) Boquillas Canyon, the longest of the three major canyons of the Rio Grande, on the eastern side of Big Bend National Park, and (bottom) the rocky, barren valley of the Rio Grande between Redford and Lajitas, close to the Mexican border. This page: panoramic views from Sotol Vista Overlook across the stark mountains of Big Bend National Park.

Designated the official State Flower, the Texas Bluebonnet (right) is one of over 5,000 species of wild flowers to be found in Texas. Big Bend National Park alone supports more than 1,100 plant types. These include cactii (facing page and below) and yuccas (bottom), which are well adapted to the park's arid desert regions. Bottom right: rowboats on the Rio Grande lend a sense of scale to magnificent Santa Elena Canyon, Big Bend National Park, where the canyon walls tower for 1,500 feet.

Facing page top: the distant contours of the Guadalupe Mountains silhouetted against a dramatic evening sky. Formed between 225 and 280 million years ago beneath a vast saltwater basin, they are now regarded as the world's most extensive fossil reef. Facing page bottom and above: the stark outline of El Capitan, a sheer, 2,000-foot-high cliff, the most prominent feature of Guadalupe Mountains National Park, close to the New Mexican border in southwest Texas.

27

These pages: the breathtakingly-beautiful Carlsbad Caverns, formed in a
limestone reef by percolating ground water, lie beneath the foothills of the
Guadalupe Mountains in southern New Mexico. Tinted by minerals, their
strange and delicate limestone formations have a magical, iridescent quality.
Overleaf: the remarkable Painted Desert, in north Arizona.

Within the Painted Desert (above and facing page bottom), Petrified Forest National Park (remaining pictures and overleaf) covers more than 94,000 acres of parched, barren land. The petrified remains of trees, alive about 200 million years ago and preserved as silica deposits gradually replaced the original wood tissues, lie strewn across the forbidding landscape. Overleaf: petrified logs scatter the slopes of Blue Mesa, one of six separate "forests" in Petrified Forest National Park.

These pages: petrified wood in Petrified Forest National Park, where mineral deposits have stained the silica to form beautiful, jewel-like stone (above). Abundant deposits of the wood were first recorded in the 1850s. By the turn of the century, however, excessive commercial exploitation of these natural treasures led to public concern and calls for the preservation and protection of the region. Nowadays, removal of any petrified wood from the park is prohibited, and only wood collected from areas outside the park can be sold.

Overleaf: the awesome Grand Canyon, in northwestern Arizona, seen from Yaki Point on the South Rim. Cut by the Colorado River, the Grand Canyon is the world's most intricate and complex system of canyons, gorges and ravines. It reaches a depth of one mile, is over 200 miles in length and ranges in width from four to eighteen miles. All along its length, layers of exposed rock rise majestically from the canyon floor to reveal an incredible story of erosion and upheaval spanning two billion years.

The Colorado River (above right) cuts through rock layers at a rate of six and a half inches every thousand years as it snakes west through the Grand Canyon (these pages and overleaf). Above left: a bird's-eye view of the river from the Point Sublime area, and (top) late evening light casting long shadows over the softened contours of the canyon seen from Mohave Point on the South Rim. Facing page: (top) delicate hues of buff, gray, green and pink color the otherwise stark landscape seen from Mather Point, and (bottom) sunset beyond Desert View. Minerals from an upstream spring sometimes color the Little Colorado River (overleaf) turquoise as it flows through the eastern reaches of Grand Canyon National Park to merge with the Colorado River.

The Grand Canyon (these pages and overleaf) attracts millions of visitors each year. Above: mule riders and backpackers pass crumbling cliffs overlooking Bright Angel Trail, a twisting nine-and-a-half-mile route across wild terrain, starting from the west end of Grand Canyon Village, and (facing page) a sheer outcrop in the Marble Canyon area. Overleaf: sunk among rocky cliffs, the oasis of Havasu Falls (left top) is fringed with lush vegetation. Left bottom: the Battleship viewed from Pima Point, and (right) changing light altering the mood of landscapes seen from West Rim Drive.

Though apparently bleak and barren, the Grand Canyon (previous pages) supports a rich diversity of plant and animal life, with over 1,000 kinds of flowering plants (these pages) bringing a vivid splash of color to the desert. Surrounded by sun-parched cliffs, the waters of Havasu Creek pour over a rocky ledge into a clear blue pool below to form Havasu Falls (overleaf), the second of three major waterfalls to be found downstream from Supai village in Havasupai Indian Reservation. Following pages: (left) the Colorado River winds its way through the Grand Canyon, and (right) rowboats on the Colorado accentuate the immense scale of Marble Canyon, named by John Wesley Powell on his historic expedition down the river in 1869. The rock he took to be polished marble is actually limestone, sandstone and shale.

Previous pages: the Grand Canyon seen from the Colorado River. The powerful Virgin River carries three million tons of rock annually downstream to its confluence with the Colorado. This adds to its erosive force as it cuts its valley through Zion National Park (these pages and overleaf), a strange land of towering rock formations, deep, narrow canyons and broad mesas. Facing page: (top) the Court of the Patriarchs, and (bottom) a panoramic view from Canyon Overlook. Top: East Temple, (above) Angels Landing and (overleaf) the Sentinel.

Bryce Canyon National Park (these pages and overleaf), southwestern Utah, is set in high country ranging from 8,000 to 9,000 feet above sea level and actually comprises a series of 12 large amphitheaters rather than a canyon. The park was named for Ebenezer Bryce, an early Mormon settler of Scottish descent, who seemed unimpressed by the grandeur of his magical surroundings. To him, Bryce Canyon was simply "a hell of a place to lose a cow!" For most visitors, however, the emotional response is one of awe and reverence. The bizarre and beautiful rock formations of Bryce Canyon National Park have been sculptured almost entirely by water, in the form of heavy rains, snow and ice. The process began some 60 million years ago when layers of sediment were deposited by inland lakes and seas. Powerful pressures from within the earth subsequently forced the land upwards to create distinct plateaus of alternate layers of relatively hard and soft rock. Over the centuries, water acted as an erosive force on these tablelands to produce the fantastic spires, arches and towers seen today. The delicacy of these rock formations is enhanced by their colors. Iron oxides, manganese and copper have combined to create a multitude of different shades, concentrations of iron producing pinks and reds and high levels of manganese tinting the rocks lavender and green. It is a landscape of everchanging moods, with the light constantly altering colors and perspectives. Facing page: rock towers and pinnacles seen from Paria View, (above) an unusual sculptured form, and (left) a natural bridge on the Navajo Loop trail. Overleaf: dramatic sunlight and shadows below Inspiration Point.

The main geological features of Bryce Canyon National Park (these pages) can be viewed easily from the 35-mile-long rim road. The park is best seen, however, on foot or on horseback from one of the many trails leading down to the canyon floor. Facing page: (top) craggy rock formations along Navajo Loop trail and (bottom) Natural Bridge. This page: warmly-colored rock spires along Queen's Garden trail.

Visitors to Bryce Canyon National Park (these pages) enter a world of fantasy.
Top: sunlight lends warmth to clustered stone pillars seen from Inspiration
Point. The Paiute Indians aptly described such limestone and sandstone
formations as "red rocks standing like men in a bowl-shaped canyon."
Throughout the park, the rock has been sculptured into amazing shapes and
forms. Above: red-stained Balanced Rock, (facing page top) orange outcrops in
Agua Canyon, and (facing page bottom) yellow ramparts below Sunset Point.

Above: naturally-formed ramparts fortify Gulliver's Castle in Queen's Garden, (facing page) a Douglas fir tree, hemmed in by rocky cliffs, reaches for the sky, and (overleaf) the evening sun catches one of the peaks at Paria View, all in Bryce Canyon.

Isolated and not easily accessible, much of Capitol Reef National Park (these pages and overleaf), in southern Utah, remains a rugged wilderness. The tilted cliff face of Capitol Reef itself rises 1,000 feet above the Fremont River and extends for 20 miles. It forms part of the Waterpocket Fold, a dramatic and geologically-unique fold of colorful rock layers almost 100 miles long. Facing page: (top) a textured rock face seen through the arch of Hickman Bridge, and (bottom) the Narrows, in Capitol Gorge, where the walls rise to 1,000 feet and narrow to about 18 feet. Above: Eph Hanks Tower, named for an early pioneer and leader in the Mormon Church, and (overleaf) Chimney Rock, its cap of hard rock slowing the erosion of the softer rock beneath.

Pyramids, cliffs and monoliths appear in countless shapes and rich colors in Capitol Reef National Park (these pages). Capitol Reef was named for its characteristic, rounded "capitol" domes weathered from Navajo Sandstone. The word "reef" simply denotes a barrier, Capitol Reef having posed great problems to early travelers seeking a path through the area. In this untamed landscape, wind and water have chiseled fine patterns and textures into rock formations such as Twin Rocks (above) and Pectol Pyramid (facing page bottom).

Above: the Egyptian Temple, and (top) Cassidy Arch, both in Capitol Reef National Park. The natural forces of erosion, in the form of running water, wind, rain, frost and sun, have also relentlessly carved fantastic rock sculptures in Arches National Park (remaining pictures), southeastern Utah. Facing page: Delicate Arch, standing in lonely splendor on the brink of a canyon, and (left) South Window.

The arches, windows, pinnacles and pedestals of Arches National Park (these pages and overleaf) are part of a dynamic, continuing story of geological evolution that began some 150 million years ago. Sand laid down mainly by wind was buried by further deposits before gradually hardening to form Entrada Sandstone. Much later, this 300-foot layer was exposed once more as a result of erosion, and a lengthy process of weathering began which has sculpted the park's distinctive formations. Above: a twisted, weather-beaten tree accentuates the drama of Devils Garden, and (right) the immense span of North Window frames Turret Arch. Sharply silhouetted against the evening sky, Delicate Arch (facing page top) is the most famous landmark in a park dominated by massive rock formations. Monumental vertical slabs, 150 to 300 feet high, line the narrow corridor of South Park Avenue (facing page bottom), and (overleaf) the huge stone arcs of Double Arch dwarf a solitary figure beneath.

The harsh terrain of Canyonlands National Park (these pages and overleaf), southeastern Utah, surrounds the confluence of the Colorado and Green rivers. These two major rivers have carved up the Colorado Plateau into a wilderness of sandstone spires, canyons and mesas, an inhospitable and unyielding region for all but the most adaptable plants and animals. Facing page: sunlight enhances the warm colors of the rock on a trail (top) near Peekaboo Spring and at Squaw Flat (bottom), in the spectacular Needles area (above and overleaf) at the southern end of the park.

Carved away by the Green River on the west and the Colorado River on the east, the Island in the Sky (facing page top) rises in the center of Canyonlands National Park (these pages and overleaf) to command spectacular views across a forbidding landscape. Facing page bottom: the dramatic scenery of the Colorado River, and (top) rocky outcrops in the Needles area, where weathering and jointing have created red and white banded spires (above). Overleaf: raft trips along the Colorado River remain a popular visitor attraction.

The spectacular beauty of Canyonlands National Park (previous pages, these pages and overleaf) derives from the harsh climate that makes it so inhospitable. Daily, as well as seasonal, temperature changes can be extreme, whilst rainfall, usually in the form of brief summer thundershowers, amounts to less than ten inches a year. Salt Creek (previous pages) drains much of the Needles area at the southern end of the park before merging with the Colorado River. Although the rugged terrain of Canyonlands appears desolate and empty, it supports an abundance of plant and animal life. Numerous species of cactii (these pages) are found here, their vividly-colored flowers brightening the arid landscape. Overleaf: the delicate flowers of the western peppergrass bloom in profusion below the Wooden Shoe.

Mesa Verde National Park (these pages and overleaf), in the southwestern tip of Colorado, occupies a green tableland area rising 1,500 feet above the surrounding valleys. Ancient cliff dwellings up to 13 centuries old, skilfully constructed on the cliff ledges and in the caves, give a fascinating insight into an elaborate Indian settlement mysteriously abandoned about 600 years ago. Below: Square Tower House, backed by the sheer wall of Navajo Canyon, and (bottom and overleaf) Cliff Palace, the largest and most famous cliff dwelling, built under the protection of a high, vaulted cave roof.

With numerous high peaks exceeding 10,000 feet and around 40 miles of the Continental Divide running through it, Rocky Mountain National Park (these pages and overleaf) is often referred to as the "top of the continent." Over a period of some 60 million years the land has been lifted by volcanic activity, eroded by the elements, and cut by great glaciers to its present shape. Above: the brilliant blue waters of Bear Lake, backed by Long Peak, and (facing page) autumn sunlight filtering through the golden leaves of aspen trees. Overleaf: Flat Top Mountain.

Established in 1915 to protect and preserve a region of outstanding beauty,
Rocky Mountain National Park (these pages and overleaf) covers an area of
263,000 acres. Top and facing page: groves of silver-barked aspen, and (above)
magnificent mountain scenery mirrored in the still waters of Bear Lake.
Overleaf: tranquil Beaver Ponds in Hidden Valley.

The snow-covered peaks of Grand Teton National Park (previous pages, these pages and overleaf), northwestern Wyoming, rise 7,000 feet above the nearby Snake River valley. The blue-gray Tetons, a young mountain range by geological standards, are a fine example of the fault-block type of mountain. Powerful subterranean pressures forced up the land along a fault to expose a huge block of the earth's crust. The western half tilted upwards and the eastern half sank, accounting for the steep eastern face of the Grand Tetons and their gentle western slopes. Water, wind and frost sculptured the mountain mass, and glaciers subsequently deepened the canyons and scoured out the moraine lakes. Established in 1929, Grand Teton is an exceptional wildlife sanctuary and one of America's most popular national parks. Hiking, horseback riding, fishing, boating, mountaineering and skiing are among a wide range of recreational activities available to visitors here. Jackson Lake (previous pages, above and facing page bottom), edged by coniferous forests and overlooked by majestic mountains, is the largest body of water in the area. Right: the clear waters of Jenny Lake, and (facing page top) Snake River winding through forests of pine, spruce and fir.

Extending into southern Montana and eastern Idaho from northwestern Wyoming, Yellowstone National Park (these pages and overleaf) is the largest and best known national park in America. The park is famous for its ten thousand geysers, hot springs, mud volcanoes and fumaroles, making it the most extensive thermal area in the world. Yellowstone is also unequaled as a wildlife sanctuary, with fish-filled lakes and rivers frequented by many varieties of waterfowl, and rugged mountains with forest-covered slopes inhabited by a wide range of mammals. Moose wander in the wetlands and ospreys soar and wheel over the canyons of this high mountain plateau, established as the first national park in 1872 to protect and preserve more than two million acres of awe-inspiring mountain wilderness. Right: Castle Geyser in Upper Geyser Basin, and (below) Abyss Pool in West Thumb Geyser Basin. Facing page: (top) the silver waters of Gibbon River, and (bottom) Firehole River snaking through steaming Midway Geyser Basin. Overleaf: seen from Artist Point, the Yellowstone River plunges 309 feet over Lower Falls into the canyon below.

Successive volcanic eruptions and the sculpting forces of glacial ice and running water have combined to create the fascinating landscape of Yellowstone National Park (these pages and overleaf). Facing page: the frothing white waters of Kepler Cascades tumble down a hillside, and (above) the Yellowstone River thunders over Lower Falls. Overleaf: Firehole River, warmed by the hot springs in its bed, calmly flows through Midway Geyser Basin.

Yellowstone National Park (these pages and overleaf) is renowned for its extensive hydrothermal features. Below: Castle Geyser, thought to be the oldest geyser in Yellowstone, and (bottom) Black Sand Basin. Most of the colors of the pools and springs are due to bacteria, algae and minerals in the hot water. Facing page: (top) Cistern Spring in Norris Geyser Basin, and (bottom) Scaup Lake surrounded by snow-laden trees. Overleaf: (left) Emerald Pool in Black Sand Basin, and (right) Lower Falls, seen from Artist Point.

The wild mountain country of Yellowstone National Park (previous pages, these pages and overleaf) is spectacular throughout the year. Previous pages: the Yellowstone River cascading over Lower Falls, (top) Minerva Terrace, formed from travertine, at Mammoth Hot Springs, and (above) Midway Geyser Basin. Facing page: (top) bison at Black Sand Basin and (bottom) Morning Glory Pool, named for its resemblance to the morning glory flower. Overleaf: the Upper Falls of the Yellowstone River.

Glacier National Park (these pages and overleaf), northwestern Montana, was established in 1920 to preserve over one million acres of magnificent Rocky Mountain wilderness. This landscape was formed over millions of years, as a series of changes thrust one edge of part of the earth's crust upward and over another and then streams and glaciers carved the mountains, cirques and valleys. Above: a dramatic view of St. Mary Lake and (facing page) Fusillade Mountain. Overleaf: (left top) Swiftcurrent Lake, (right top) Mount Sinopah seen beyond the shores of Two Medicine Lake, and (right bottom) a panoramic view from Logan Pass, the highest point along Going-to-the-Sun Road.

136

The outstanding scenery of Glacier National Park (these pages, overleaf and following page) is most accessible during the summer months. Top: waterfall in Sunrift Gorge, (right) the frothing waters of Avalanche Creek on the Trail of the Cedars, and (facing page) Logan Creek Falls. Overleaf: the imposing face of Garden Wall towering above McDonald Creek, and (following page) heavy skies over the clear waters of Bowman Lake.